16/2

A NORTHERN SPRING

FRANK ORMSBY

A Northern Spring

SECKER & WARBURG
LONDON

THE GALLERY PRESS
DUBLIN

First published in England 1986 by
Martin Secker & Warburg Limited
54 Poland Street, London WIV 3DF
and in Ireland 1986 by
The Gallery Press,
19 Oakdown Road, Dublin 14

British Library Cataloguing in Publication Data

Ormsby, Frank
A northern spring.
I. Title
821.914   PR6065.R69

ISBNs 0–436–34100–X (UK)

0 904011 92 5 paper (Ireland)
0 904011 93 3 cloth

The Gallery Press receives financial
assistance from The Arts Council/An
Chomhairle Ealaíon, Ireland

Typeset by Inforum Ltd, Portsmouth
Printed in Great Britain by
Redwood Burn Ltd, Trowbridge

For
My Mother
Anne Jane Ormsby

ACKNOWLEDGEMENTS

Acknowledgements are due to the following: *Agni Review* (USA); *Aquarius*; BBC Radio Ulster; *Encounter*; *Fortnight*; *Gown*; *Krino*; *New Statesman*; *North Magazine*; *Observer*; *Paris/Atlantic* (France); *Poetry Ireland Review*; *Poetry Review*; *Times Literary Supplement*; *Trimestrial Poetry Review* (Belgium). 'The Bees' Nest' appeared in the pamphlet *Being Walked by a Dog* (Ulsterman Publications, 1978). 'Incurables' won a prize in the 1979 National Poetry Competition.

Some of the poems in 'A Northern Spring' include details borrowed or adapted from a number of books about World War II and its effects, most notably *V Was for Victory: Politics and American Culture During World War II* by John Morton Blum, *The Battle for Normandy* by Eversley Belfield and H. Essame and *WWII* by James Jones.

I am similarly indebted to *Miracle on the River Kwai* by Ernest Gordon and *The Burma-Siam Railway: The Secret Diary of Dr Robert Hardie 1942–45* for some of the details in 'The Diary'.

CONTENTS

Travelling   1
The Diary   2
Felix Peccione's *Crucifixion*   3
A Northern Spring
   1 *The Clearing*   4
   2 *McConnell's Birthday*   5
   3 *Cleo, Oklahoma*   6
   4 *Lesson of the War*   7
   5 *The Padre*   8
   6 *I Died in a Country Lane*   9
   7 *Bridie*   10
   8 *I Stepped on a Small Landmine*   11
   9 *For the Record*   12
  10 *The Flame Thrower*   13
  11 *The Liberation*   14
  12 *Maimed Civilians, Isigny*   15
  13 *Apples, Normandy, 1944*   16
  14 *They Buried Me in an Orchard*   17
  15 *The Night I Lost World War II*   18
  16 *Seaplanes at Castle Archdale*   19
  17 *Grenade-Fishing in the Orne*   20
  18 *On Devenish Island*   21
  19 *Between the Lines*   22
  20 *McCook, Nebraska*   23
  21 *The Gardener's Help*   24
  22 *Duffy's Basement Bar*   25
  23 *Darkies*   26
  24 *The Convoy*   27
  25 *A Cross on a White Circle*   28
  26 *Ste-Mère-Église*   29
  27 *Return to California*   30
  28 *Dayton, Ohio*   31
  29 *After the Depression*   32
  30 *Soldier Bathing*   33
  31 *Safe Home*   34

32 *Among the Dead*   35
33 *From the German*   36
34 *My Memory Collected Places*   37
35 *Some of Us Stayed Forever*   38
36 *Postscripts*   39
Home and Away   40
News From Home   41
At the Jaffé Memorial Fountain, Botanic
  Gardens   42
My Careful Life   44
The Bees' Nest   45
Dailies   46
The War Photographers   47
Street Life
    1 *Near Windsor Park*   48
    2 *Slum Terrace*   49
    3 *Mechanics*   50
Survivors   51
Incurables   52
King William Park   53
Home   54

TRAVELLING

I

My grandmother's French journal was full of trains,
the market stalls and stately *grandes horloges* of 1890.
She sketched the beans drying under the eaves,
the sprigging of tulle in doorways, the great cheeses
of Pont L'Evêque,
and an old woman groaning paternosters
in the Rue de la Paix.

Oriels and fine vistas – her France a work
of the selective imagination, fit to grace
that Boston drawing-room,
its polished wood, cheval-glass reflecting
her passion for Europe:
porcelain from Sèvres, a quart of Bushmills
and the novels of Henry James.

II

All my grandmother's travelling was in her head.
She'd never been to Boston or to France.

She died in her Russian phase,
in the hard winter of 1913,
sunk between pillows as though she struggled through
some pass in the Caucasus –
insisting on local colour to the last stroke,
ink-stains amok on the next snowy pages.

THE DIARY

I buried it in the cemetery at Chungkai,
two rolls of jotter in a Thermos flask
filched from the Raffles College at Singapore,
and dug it up in 1945
on a daytrip from Bangkok.

So much I had forgotten, sights and sounds
of a year in the jungle:
lime trees and red chillis growing wild
at the edge of the compounds, cicadas, jungle frogs,
the cool poignance of the evening bell
from the Italian mission.

So much remembered: Tamils and Javanese
buried by the hundred, barges piled with dead
nudging downstream from Ninety-kilometre Camp,
the endless epidemics, the brutish guard
snarling 'Speedo! Speedo!'

And, regular as on a timetable, page by page,
the names of the first stations:
the cemetery at Tarsoe,
the cemetery at Ban Pong,
the cemetery at Chungkai.

FELIX PECCIONE'S *CRUCIFIXION*

St Malachy's, Alfred Street, Belfast

Autumnal bass of *Umbria*,
passionate lilt of *Trasimeno*:
sounds in the mouths of exiles, naming home
between the Lough and York Street,
the year that Garibaldi marched on Rome.

How a mural hung for decades
in the same alcove,
blent with the church patterns of light, shadow,
ornament, begins, like my *Crucifixion*,
to resemble a fresco.

Closer, you will meet the unsettled eyes
of the soldier following instructions.
He turns an alien head
and God only knows what he thinks of the thunderous sky
or events at the centre:
a Roman in exile, earning his daily bread.

A NORTHERN SPRING

1 THE CLEARING

Remote as home and Europe, the broken sounds
drift to me through the laurels, miles from the compound.
Sporadic practice battles. Behind the lodge,
McConnell's axe is attacking another tree.
The manor car glides by on the avenue.

Bluebells and crocuses and saplings' wings.
We came with the Spring. They say our time will come
in the third month, before the Spring is over.
My hammock sways to the swing of a faint march
on distant gravel.

Here is a place I will miss with a sweet pain,
as I miss you always, perhaps because I was spared
the colourless drag of its winter. This is an hour
to dream again the hotel room where we changed
from the once-worn, uncreased garments,

assured and beside ourselves and lonely-strange.

2 McCONNELL'S BIRTHDAY

My father died among the Guinchy brickstacks
in the First War, before I was seventeen.
Daily I stopped to read his weathered name
on the dull statue in the village square
until I forgot him.

I worked the manor farm, my children grew
in a green place at the foot of the Major's trees.
The year that Bridie left they filled my days,
riding the tractor to the stable yard.
We were closer when she returned.

I've no urge to watch how the world goes,
or cry for the century and its latest war.
At forty-four I'm up with the first light
to feed the Major's pheasants.
I close his gates at night.

Today there are shouts on the road, McCusker's boy
going home from the creamery, Donnelly taking his time
on a creaky bike. Slyly he stops to roar:
'We're not getting any younger.'
In this part of the world they know it's my birthday.

3 CLEO, OKLAHOMA

'I knew he'd be a big shot.' My mother's words,
in the third person, as though I'd already gone.
She stepped back through shadows, relinquished me
to sun and bunting, a street of cheers and smiles
from there to the depot. The Mayor struck a pose
for a possible statue,

but the bandsmen stayed in tune until I waved
from the steps of the Greyhound. Already I belonged
to somewhere else, or nowhere, or the next
photograph. The Mayor spread his arms
and had trouble with History.

There was dust everywhere. It was too late to cry
or too early. I heard the Mayor say:
'We've had History before now, folks, in this town.
There'll be more History soon.'

4 LESSON OF THE WAR

I wish this war was over. The other day,
walking from school, I climbed the big oak tree
on the lough shore to watch for aeroplanes.
That was when I saw her, Eileen McConnell
lying with some airman at the foot of a field.
They rolled in their bare skins and gave a cry
and then stopped fighting.

My da was in bad humour when I told.
'Just like her mother,' he said and gave me a skite
and warned me to stay away from girls and soldiers.

I wish this war, this *fuckin'* war, was over.

5 THE PADRE

I

We won't forget the padre in a hurry,
his big Norton pummelling the backroads.
He roars from among the laurels,
God's batman in oils and goggles,
or strides into pub brawls with sweet crosses,
calling for peace.

The padre has no special voice for prayer.
His talk is the right words for broken men
and village children,
Schulz in the sick-bay, anonymous with fear,
and little Goering, brooding on his name.

II

Meatpackers, truckers, longshoremen from Maine,
Slav lumberjacks, tough immigrants at home
on the wharves of the East River,
a Negro lad who lied about his age
in Jackson, Missouri.

On a wall outside the compound they have composed
their own exile's prayer, a dense litany
of half the towns in the Union:
Battle Creek, Michigan to Broken Bow,
Dripping Springs, Texas to Woodstock, Vermont.

My congregations.
All in uniform.
All in a strange country, passing through.

6 I DIED IN A COUNTRY LANE

I died in a country lane near Argentan,
my back to a splintered poplar,
my eyes on fields
where peace had not been broken
since the Hundred Years War.
And a family returned to the farm
at the end of the lane.
And Patton sent his telegram: 'Dear Ike,
today I spat in the Seine.'
And before nightfall Normandy was ours.

7 BRIDIE

A cry breaks on the landing, escaped from a dream.
It sinks, complete, too swiftly to be named
as pain or pleasure, till its echo breaks
deeply in me. I know it as a cry
of love and sorrow: an abandoned cry.

The wind that tears the arms from sycamores
was loose in the plantation the night I ran.
Once, in a stormy tunnel, a stunned bat
blundered against me. Blind with thundery rain
I fell on stone. Blood drained from my side.

I ran for love. They hunted me with drums,
those stricken hearts. Above the swarming gale
he turned in his sleep. Their sighs were deafening.
That night and many nights I heard them breathe
harsher than storm. Cries from the lips of wounds.

The love I fled for perished in a year,
though words were spoken. Haunting the house of loss,
I drove love from me. Love was not to blame.
'It's for the best,' John said, 'you'll settle now,'
and took me in. Maybe he was not wrong.

The pheasants peck at their netting. Nothing disturbs
the compound outside the window where they are reared
to panic between the beaters and the guns;
for gunfire patterns the distance, no longer worth
a fluttering leap, the lift of a startled head.

Sleepless tonight, I cherish any breeze
that sweeps the plantation, clears the plantation wall.
Old thunder brattles faintly, mumbling still
of one blinded by lightning who lives to see
a milder twilight. It aches in my stippled scar.

I stepped on a small landmine in the *bocage*
and was spread, with three others, over a field
of burnt lucerne.
The bits they shipped to Georgia at the request
of my two sisters were not entirely me.
If dead men laughed, I would have laughed the day
the committee for white heroes honoured me,
and honoured too the mangled testicles
of Leroy Earl Johnson.

When I stabbed a Belfast gigolo at the Plaza
they transferred me to the country to cool down.
There were no poolrooms or waterfront hotels,
just woods, cows, a village, flat fields
and enough fresh air to poison a city boy.
And when the MPs kicked me senseless in Duffy's Bar
for being a 'wise guy', I burned their quarters down
one night in May with gas from their own jeeps
and they could prove nothing.
Cornered at St-Marcouf, I shot my way
to a medal and commendation (posthumous),
a credit at last to my parents, whoever they were,
and the first hero produced by the State Pen.

We were all in the lap of the gods, as Smokey said,
an unpredictable, tumescent place.
You might be dandled there or due a caress
or fucked quick as lightning if your tree camouflage
wasn't just right.
His own lightning never struck less than twice,
the woods in front of him a melting waste
of real and human trees.

On the road to Pont L'Abbé we met a man
with his wife in a wheelbarrow,
a blanketful of belongings under her chin
like a monstrous goitre.
Wobbling from occupied France, their faces set
against indignity,
between the fires of Pont L'Abbé and the fresh ruins
of Chef du Pont,
they stopped at the roadside, stiff with courtesy,
and suffered their liberation.

12 MAIMED CIVILIANS, ISIGNY

We did not see the wreckage or hear the cries.
The train had stopped smoking around its dead
somewhere back in the tunnel, the planes had gone
when we got to the tunnel entrance and found them there,
civilian casualties from the core of disaster.

We thought of ourselves and chose to think of them
as grounds for optimism:
the men would master crutches, the bandaged girls
marry in wheelchairs.

First words, first rites, the work of consolation,
Calvados and chocolate on their scorching tongues.

Was it D+10 or D+12 we caught
the war artist sketching apples?

'I'm sick of tanks,' he said. 'I'm sick of ruins.
I'm sick of dead soldiers and soldiers on the move
and soldiers resting.
And to tell you the truth, I'm sick drawing refugees.
I want to draw apples.'

For all we know he's still sitting under a tree
somewhere between the Seine and Omaha,
or, russet with pleasure, striding past old dugouts
towards the next windfall –
sketch-books accumulating as he becomes
the Audubon of French apples,

or works on the single apple
– perfect, planetary – of his imagination.

They buried me in an orchard at St Lô
on a pillaged farm. For twelve months I lay
under leaves and ripe windfalls, the thin roots
pressing me, fingering me, till I let them through.
They dug me up and buried me again
one June morning to a roll of drums
in a plain box on the ninety-seventh row
of an immaculate war cemetery.
If anything is left of me, it lives
in Ruth, Nevada, where my people farm
in spite of dust and drought, in spite of my death,
or a small town in Ireland where a child
carries my name, though he may never know
that I was his father.

How do you lose a war? I'll tell you how.

Parachuting after dark, I almost drowned
in the Vire estuary,
stumbled half the night
through woods, cornfields, clover, country lanes,
so far off course the maps were useless.
I looked down one grey road after another
but the war was not to be found.

At dawn the war found me, asleep in a barn.
The first man in the regiment to see the Rhine,
I starved in Bavaria for another year
as a guest of the Wehrmacht.

Then home to Nebraska without firing a round.

16 SEAPLANES AT CASTLE ARCHDALE

Insects tick in the tarmac, brisk relays
next to our feet at the fringe of a cratered road.
We climb through wire, the slope to the lough shore
so thick with buttercups we hardly dare
our feet among them. Jake, the labrador,
lopes to the water, snuffing the scents of Spring.

Somewhere beyond the island's screen of trees
the runways rumble. He laughs at my unease
and folds his uniform so that the wings
are uppermost and seem to catch the sun:
still butterflies. All afternoon we lie
on a plaid blanket.

Through half-closed eyes I scan the inscrutable sky.

Grenade-fishing in the Orne – a far cry
from tickling trout in Utah at seventeen,
or lines trailed from the footbridge of a stream
clean off the mountains.
The fish rolled to the surface, shock in their eyes,
a river-plague, a sickly visitation.

They flew me back to Utah with shock in my eyes,
that rimmed and frozen look the marines call
the two-thousand-yard-stare.
The bridges are all targets now, the pools
belch like a hot springs and dead faces
balloon to the surface.
The dark flies glisten, the faces bloom in the sun.

We rowed from Trory on a lough so clear
that even the loughside cows, as Milburn said,
had waded out to stand in their reflections.
Weiss from Milwaukee manned the second oar,
and Pedersen the Slav had trained his lens
on the round tower.

That was a lazy Sunday among the ruins.
When we flicked ash into the saint's stone bed,
or pitched our baseball through the perfect arch
of a church window's crumbling Romanesque,
we meant no harm, the past completed there
was not affected.

It was twilight when we returned. Drifting to sleep
in the hut's darkness I thought of how we had strayed
through empty fields next to the cemetery,
our wake settling before we had reached the shore.

Les sanglots longs des violons de l'automne

Locked in a dark storeroom at Bayeux,
a chemist hears at last the long-drawn sad
first cadence of Verlaine's *Chanson d'Automne*.
He hides his radio and begins to prepare.

At Pont L'Evêque the line runs in the head
of a railway porter. At Arromanches a clerk
carries it through the blackout to the ears
of the priest's housekeeper.

And the big troopships gather on the English coast,
in Belfast Lough. It is the first of June.
Five days and nights the Channel airwaves listen
for the second line:

20 McCOOK, NEBRASKA

At ease on the banks of the Republican
the three months I duck through Europe.
My mother draws the curtains. This week, again,
the streets are empty of uniforms, no one like me
is crouched on her veranda.
Thousands of miles from Cherbourg and Falaise
the log schoolhouse, the Congregational Church
are in no one's sights but my father's.
He cleans his glasses, prepares to read aloud
what's been happening abroad, the latest news
of war in Europe, war in the Pacific, war on the Eastern Front.

He has no eye for butterflies, their soft
crash in the flowers. If his hands were free
to touch his cap,
he would not take the time
when the manor car glides by on the avenue.

His father's axe falls with a muted thud –
less than an echo where his billhook clears
a space for planting.
All afternoon his grievances are aimed
deep in the brambles.

Beyond the trees the distances are mined
with blasts and tremors, the rifle-range expends
its lethal chatter. Vapours sharpen the air:
woodsmoke and cordite, the drifting troubled haze
of smoke on Johnstone's quarry, where his friends

are earning more and learning to use explosives.

22 DUFFY'S BASEMENT BAR

In Duffy's Basement Bar on Saturdays
the 'blanket' Indian, Silas Clinton Jones,
unhinged with whiskey,
challenges all palefaces to fight
Birch Coolie, White Stone Hill, Dead Buffalo Lake,
the Minnesota Sioux Wars of '62.
No takers and a lot of straight faces
till the MPs have bundled him away.

More dangerous the bottled, sullen burn,
day-in, day-out:
meatball, kike, sambo, waiting his turn.

23 DARKIES

They called themselves the North Fermanagh Branch
of the Brotherhood of Sleeping Car Porters:
Ben Champion, Lester Coleman, Burton Bazanne
escaped for the day from the Quartermaster Corps
to cycle the backroads,
the first 'darkies' anyone could remember
in this part of the world.

In May they disappeared, their blood perhaps
acceptable at last to spill in France
or fill a Red Cross bottle. Long after, I recall
their voices raised in bitterness in Ma Kerr's
unsegregated tea-shop, their mock harmonies
on *Ol' Man River*, the *Chocolate Soldiers* song.

24 THE CONVOY

Miss McCamley's Raleigh toils uphill,
the handlebars unsteerable with shopping.
She slumps on a stone with barely breath to wheeze
'I'm not worth thruppence. God, I haven't a puff.'
shields the third match and lights a tiny dune
of Potter's Asthma Remedy.
A hiss of pungent smoke, a wincing sound.
The convoy passes.

A cross on a white circle marked a church
and a cross on a black circle a calvary.
Reading the map too hastily we advanced
to the wrong village and so had gone too far
and were strafed by our own fighters.
In the time it takes to tell Bretteville sur Laize
from Bretteville le Rabet, twelve of us died.

26 STE-MÈRE-EGLISE

The church was a nest of snipers. For three hours
we crouched in courtyards, crawled in a cobbled square
from cover to cover. The people had hidden or fled.
Baedeker never saw Ste-Mère-Eglise
the way we did.

Next year I'll make a pilgrimage in long shorts
with camera, sandals and a shirt so loud
the French will need sunglasses.
Just once I'll say a prayer and walk upright
through every street. Afterwards there will be time

for wine, for souvenirs, for war museums.

'They live like rats, breed like rats and act
like rats. We don't want them.'
The week of Pearl Harbor their shops burned
and the Tushiba boy was trampled to death.
Our barber offered 'free shaves to Japs'
but was 'not responsible for accidents'.

How much has changed? The township still belongs
to the Native Sons and Daughters of the Golden West.

The barber sings because the streets are free
of Orientals – though there are blacks and Jews.

Three weeks, the papers say, should be enough
for 'oppressive remembering'.

I watch for them in the mornings. If they are free
they slip from the rhododendrons. George takes the reins,
Chuck rolls cheroots and hunkers on the boards
among my father's milk-cans.
The cart squeals on, they read to me as we go:
letters from home, the girls of Dayton, Ohio.

In the light evenings, when we kneel to pray,
my mother watches me. Her face is sad.
She hears, through murmured sleepy litanies,
names from a scuffed atlas drum in my head:
Gdansk, Archangel and lately, like a slow
train in a distant tunnel, Dayton, Ohio.

'The man who relaxes is helping the Axis'
was the poem on everyone's lips in Ford County.
And the country got up early and went to work.
And Hitler smirked from the back of the toilet door
on the factory shirkers.

Frost-bitten in Bastogne, I blessed the hands
that sewed my blankets, gave thanks every day
for the can of Blue Ribbon somebody stole
from the camp warehouse,
for Wrigley's Spearmint gum and my bottle of Quink.

The war made people rich in Ford County,
getters and spenders. I think I'll never warm
to the brash place they've built there, their boomtown world
of the two-car family, the electric dream-kitchen
and the Nash Kelvinator fridge.

The bigger fish have country cousins here.
At their own depth sonaghen and gillaroo
dart in the quiet loughs and are not found elsewhere.

I dry on the shore and imagine the world renewed
cleanly between two islands I cannot name:
as a rounded stone, say, that the ebb left bare,
or light on water the morning after a war.

They returned before nightfall,
a rising thrum
re-entering the silence,
forms bellying low
over the flat farms.

It was a surfacing.
We saw them clear
at the cockpit windows.

Then jeeps on the concrete,
voices, a smoky warmth
of evening breath,
the jittery gusto of men restored to the earth.

32 AMONG THE DEAD

In the cemetery on the cliffs at Omaha,
a bronze statue: the Spirit of American Youth
rising from the sea.
And the bronze urns in the loggia depict the Lord
on the face of the waters.
Memorials in Breton granite, Vaurian stone,
Pyrenean marble,
and a pavement of beach pebbles.

There were two score of ours among the dead
on the first day, none older than twenty.
Grease-monkeys, farmhands, hash slingers, their names are rare
between the town registers of Birth and Death.
They look out of school photographs where their promise
has turned to a yellowing of unfinished lives.

When I delivered the grenade cleanly through the slit
of the gun emplacement,
I buried my face in seaweed and covered my ears.

Today, forty years after, I hear it explode
in a wheelchair-veteran's book of reminiscences
'translated from the German',
and know for the first time what ended there:
Walter's dyspepsia, Heinrich's insufferable snores,
big Hofmann's correspondence course in Engineering.

And tonight, oddly alive to me as they never were,
though forty years dead, elusively they rise
to baffle grief with an inviolable presence,
some treacherous gift of innocence restored
I cannot believe in and would not refuse.

My memory collected places and carried them home
to Butte, Montana:
those Northern villages where I thought of death
and clung to living more than before or after –
Lison, Isigny, rising through the dawns
of a dangerous summer,
Irvinestown, Kesh, Ederney on the face of the earth.

Some of us stayed forever, under the lough
in the guts of a Flying Fortress,
sealed in the buckled capsule, or dispersed
with odds and ends – propellers, dogtags, wings,
a packet of Lucky Strike, the instructor's gloves –
through an old world of shells and arrowheads,
dumped furniture, a blind Viking prow.
In ten years or a hundred we will rise
to foul your nets with crushed fuselage.
Our painted stork, nosing among the reeds
with a bomb in its beak, will startle you for a day.

36 POSTSCRIPTS

I
Stars on the hill-farms. Night-smells of Spring.
The gargle of Mulligan's tractor cresting a lane,
bound for Orion.

A tap-dance from little Goering. Milburn sang.
Kalinsky sketched our last game of cards
in McConnell's kitchen.

We posed in the lamplight, studies for the walls
of the Always in My Heart Club of Cedar Rapids.

II
A litter of blanks, a rubble of rusted cans,
our curved huts in farmyards filled with hens,
the whorl of an air-raid shelter through a bank
of ferns and briars.
In a wood that is not home there is no pain
to think how we'll be forgotten.

These are my last pictures: in a trench
with Chuck and Harvey, by the pheasant-pen
behind the gate-lodge. The dark one with the gun
is Dan McConnell. Keep them. When I return
they'll fill an album. We could call it *Spring*,
or *Spring in Ireland, 1944, My Northern Spring*.

HOME AND AWAY

I

The lough has summer languages, a Berlitz school
of yachts and cruisers talking to the shore
at Castle Archdale.
On jetties where the Catalinas fuelled
for the Battle of the Atlantic
the voices these days are mostly cheerful German.
Fraulein in wetsuits gleam on the *Loreleifels*
of Davy's Island.

II

Some fishermen from Brackwede, the twin town
of Enniskillen,
have challenged the locals to a six-a-side
in the marina car-park.
Their tongues, beyond maps and commerce, ring in the sun.
And suddenly, home and away, I am ghosting through towns
of the Teutoburg Forest:
Harsewinkel, Isselhorst, Steinhagen;
the light on the lough's face is Westphalian,
the breath at the pierhead Europe's aggregate air.

NEWS FROM HOME

Quare weather we're having,
even for the time of year.
You don't know what you're missing.

That bright postcard landing in my hall
from the hottest July day
in Met. Office memory
has set me inventing again
the place I remember
as a lull between showers,
a cavern of imminent rains,
its rarities all of water:
the gillaroo
in the bowl of Lough Melvin,
the colony of grey lag geese
on Castle Coole's Palladian reflection.
Or of dark air:
I heard a year ago
of a great bat sunk
in the caves of Boho
whose kind have hung
there since the 1880's,
their shrouded, blind faces
blinking awake
in the unimaginable peace
of rumoured extinction.

But now, you say, for the first recorded time
in ninety summers –
the sun somehow just right,
the breeze in favour –
a Purple Hairstreak
has landed in Pubble Forest:
quercusia quercus,
opening on the boughs
like a tremulous winged blossom.

AT THE JAFFÉ MEMORIAL FOUNTAIN,
BOTANIC GARDENS

1

Lipman and Cohen, butchers, Hercules Lane,
Manuel Lightfoot, Smithfield, 'taylor and Jew'.
Names in the old leases, gone to ground
since the year the first sailing ships from Europe
breezed up the lough.

Wolff, Jaffé, Weinberg, purposeful merchant Jews
of Hamburg and Jessnitz. Later the refugees
on sleepless treks from places where they had grown
and spoke the language,
who improvised a style of making do
from trunks and travelling bags and the will to prosper.

2
What might they leave their children,
the dead Jews of Lübeck, Lublin,
packed in Antrim clay?
Faith and unhappy memories?
The desert flower that blooms after loss,
its red heart colouring obstinately against the urge,
insistent, inward, of the petals' bordering dark:
griefs not to be assuaged, the carrier blood's
murmur of vengeance?

3
A wind off the Lagan strays across open ground
at the Jaffé Memorial Fountain.
Half summerhouse, half temple, a room without walls,
its tenants river-smells, in-transit birds,
the dung-and-sawdust ghost of the Circus Hofmann
on a European Tour,
it stands for the ones who earned their monuments
and the ones whose lives were quiet streams hidden
for centuries in the foundations.
I think of dispersals, settlings, the random inheritors
of dispossession who kept an image of home;
of Solly Lipsitz walking his labrador
in the streets of South Belfast,
Chaim Herzog's birthplace on the Cliftonville Road.

MY CAREFUL LIFE

My careful life says: 'No surrender.
Not an inch.' Sometimes I wonder

what thrills the darkness as I pass
the scented gardens of excess

or pause in the twilight to condemn
the parked cars rocking in the lane.

But still my life cries: 'Work and save.
Rise early. Stay home after five

and pull the curtains. They are blessed
– prudent, abstemious – who resist.

All things in moderation. Share
nothing. Be seemly and austere.'

My careful life sighs: 'Love? Forget it!
Avoid what is sexually transmitted.

The "wasteful virtues", I'm afraid,
earn nothing. They put you in the red.

Samaritans get mugged. Be wise.
Pass watchfully on the other side.

Your youth was stainless. Now your joy'll
be the middle years full of self-denial,

and an old age as ripe and warm
as is commensurate with decorum.'

THE BEES' NEST

You grasped the branch.
My hands were free.
Apple nudged apple,
red and round.
Much may be shaken
from a tree.
A bees' nest tumbled
towards the ground.
I caught the nest
unerringly.

DAILIES

Twice since midnight
sudden cars have failed
to photocopy the ceiling,

we to hold –
bedded between the alley and the street –
their print of branches.

The alarm is set,
the papers that we closed
an hour ago

on grim-lipped faces,
lines of murderous eyes,
have settled in their folds

across a sideboard.
Its drawers are lined with pages from a year
we've long forgotten,

its edges cut the wallpaper to bare
a dulled newsprint
under the flowered skin.

THE WAR PHOTOGRAPHERS

Working with one eye closed or heads buried
under their drapes, they focus to preserve
the drowned shell-hole, the salient's rubble of dead,
the bleached bones of sepoys torn from the earth.

Their stills haunt us: a stretcher piled with skulls
at Cold Harbour, graves in a barren wood
that in one hour's carnage lost its name
to history and the world's memory of death.

The worst has happened, they confirm the worst:
but show us too the makeshift hospital,
the sad errand of the hospital van
among the ruins. Also enough of sky
to suggest the infinity of angles,

that behind sandbags, under the hostile towers
someone is finding time for a wry note
on bowel movements, an entry that affirms
the loved salience of what is always there:
flower of Auschwitz, bird of the Western Front.

STREET LIFE

1 NEAR WINDSOR PARK

West Bromwich two, Republic of China one,
but in Donnybrook Street the Chinese children train
for World Cup ties at the end of the century.

Slip it to Ho, the little one whose flair
prints goals on gates and gables! In embryo
the first Chinese striker in the Irish League.

2 SLUM TERRACE

Poor as Calabria. The worst housing
outside Naples. And the third grandchild comes home
to a community welcome.

All the case histories are there to sing,
with a priest, three social workers and a lorry load
of soldiers with blackened faces
mounting a search for the child's father.
The rooms are turned upside down
and inside out and the child sleeps through it –
though minutes after the priest and soldiers go,
when the boards have been nailed down with tears and curses,
he wakes to cry and cry with the other two.

The social workers stay
to walk the floor and shush them to sleep again.

3 MECHANICS

Their legs survive the carnage of garage floors,
or struggle under cars to be united
with heads and torsos.
They hang from the jaws of bonnets in a suggestion
of difficult births, resisting terrible deaths.

Upright again the mechanics purse their faces
in frowns that deny the likelihood of mending.
Their overalls the colour of corrosion,
they wring their hands in oily rags and mutter
and go on with the operation.

SURVIVORS

Sometimes they cross an avenue at dusk,
those hoarse-voiced children brashly on the move
from mews to alley.
                    Mostly they seem too young
to keep such hours and underdressed for air
that cuts its teeth on glass and barbed-wire coils,
the rusted nails of half-wrecked garages.

Rooting behind our lives for what they can find –
the bones of broken telephones, old cars
picked bare already to their oiliest springs,
dead spars along the embankment – they hug their loads
of chosen bric-à-brac and, blindly assured,
ignite with purposes: to float an ark
or point a bonfire, angle a sheet of tin
against a brick coalhouse and call it home,
or call it a tree-house.
                    As they flit from view,
their voices sack the twilight.
Their track is a littered silence where they resound.

INCURABLES

Plaques and a marble silence about the door
of the Ulster Cancer Foundation, the air a tissue
shredding between the chimneys and the moon.
We eavesdrop on police cars, the shift and crackle
of ice in the wavelengths.
Our charts are frosty promises. Their troughs
may suck us down forever and who will know
or care what perished.
Or children may have the peace
to say of us: 'They lived in troubled times.
They stayed afloat and somehow kept their warmth.'
For now, we are grateful that our breath still wreathes
east of the City Cemetery, numinous skies
between us and the troubled distances.
The blinds are lit, the moon is finding gold
in every street's mouthful of worn cobbles.

KING WILLIAM PARK

The mountains must have watched it, the startled eyes
of swamp-life and the long-shinned estuary birds:
that tidal glitter curling out to sea
for the last time, abandoning its mud.
Then centuries of minute adjustments, rivers
changing their beds,
the shifting work of sloblands under the sky
and fibrous growths toughening, holding their own.

Fowlers, fishers and settlers, intricate drains,
channels and cargoes, chimneys, streetlamps and trams;
but always the brickwork tilting, buildings on stilts,
the tide-swell echoes creeping out of the ground
yearly to meet the rainfall and shaping themselves
to crests and troughs in the tarmac, undulant cobbles.
Or pouring their excess out of sudden wounds
in streets miles inland.

Here, where the park is, breakers found a shore
to bury shells, jetsam a place to lie.
Daily the winos spend their bleary rage
in squabbles among the benches,
or sing their hearts out searching for a song
on a green patch with trees beside a junction.
And knee-capped boys on crutches raise their heads
to follow us past the railings,

wintry eyes asking how far we have come
and where we are going. A terraced marsh away,
sludge-pumps have sucked a resting-place for stone:
the blocks of a new hospital are hauled
through scaffolding, past windows where the sun
flames in the evening gloriously, or the rain
drifts into soundless networks on its way
to the earth-clogged ears in the groundwork, the listening shells.

HOME

Once, in the Giant's Ring, I closed my eyes
and thought of Ireland,
the air-wide, skin-tight, multiple meaning of here.

When I opened them I was little the wiser,
in that, perhaps, one
with the first settlers in the Lagan Valley
and the Vietnamese boat-people of Portadown.